S0-BYX-465

Badgers

and Other Mustelids

Book Author: Lisa Klobuchar
For World Book:
Editorial: Paul A. Kobasa, Scott Thomas, Christine Sullivan
Research: Cheryl Graham
Graphics and Design: Sandra Dyrlund, Brenda Tropinski
Photos: Tom Evans
Permissions: Janet Peterson
Indexing: David Pofelski
Proofreading: Tina Ramirez
Pre-press and Manufacturing: Carma Fazio, Anne Fritzinger, Steve Hueppchen

**For information about other World Book publications, visit our Web site at
http://www.worldbookonline.com or call 1-800-WORLDBK (967-5325). For information about sales
to schools and libraries, call 1-800-975-3250 (United States); 1-800-837-5365 (Canada).**

World Book, Inc.
233 N. Michigan Avenue
Chicago, IL 60601
U.S.A.

The Library of Congress has cataloged an earlier edition of this title as follows:

Badgers and other mustelids.
    p. cm. -- (World Book's animals of the world)
    Includes bibliographical references and index.
    ISBN 0-7166-1265-8
    1. Badgers--Juvenile literature. 2. Mustelidae--Juvenile literature.
    I. Title. II. World Book, Inc. III. Series.
    QL737 .C25B249 2005
    599.76'7--dc22

                         2004015690

This edition:
Badgers: ISBN-10: 0-7166-1286-0 ISBN-13: 978-0-7166-1286-5
Set 4: ISBN-10: 0-7166-1285-2   ISBN-13: 978-0-7166-1285-8

Printed in Malaysia
3 4 5 6 7 8 09 08 07

Picture Acknowledgments: Cover: © Tom Brakefield, Corbis; © D. Robert & Lorrie Franz, Corbis; © Thomas Kitchin, Tom Stack & Associates; © Gerard Lacz, Animals Animals; © Rich Reid, Animals Animals.

© Erwin & Peggy Bauer, Animals Animals 35; © Erwin & Peggy Bauer, Tom Stack & Associates 5, 53; © Peter Baumann, Animals Animals 27; © Tom Brakefield, Corbis 4, 31; © Hans Dieter Brandl, Frank Lane Picture Agency/Corbis 33; © Alan Carey, Photo Researchers 3, 17; © W. Perry Conway, Corbis 19, 21; © Michael Francis 29; © D. Robert & Lorrie Franz, Corbis 10; © John Giustina, Bruce Coleman Inc. 61; © Cathy & Gordon Illig, Animals Animals 51; © Kevin Keatley, Nature Picture Library 25; © Thomas Kitchin, Tom Stack & Associates 45, 55; © Gerard Lacz, Animals Animals 43; © Pat & Tom Leeson, Photo Researchers 39; © Zig Leszczynski, Animals Animals 57; © Joe McDonald, Tom Stack & Associates 15; © Tom Murphy, SuperStock 41; © Rich Reid, Animals Animals 37; © Juergen & Christine Sohn, Animals Animals 59; © Mark Stouffer, Animals Animals 49; © John Tinning, Frank Lane Picture Agency/Corbis 13; © Terry Whittaker, Photo Researchers 5, 47.

Illustrations: WORLD BOOK illustration by John Fleck 7. Illustration of a sett on page 23 by John Fleck, based upon research and diagrams provided by T. J. Roper, University of Sussex.

World Book's Animals of the World

Badgers
and Other Mustelids

WORLD
BOOK

a Scott Fetzer company
Chicago
www.worldbookonline.com

Contents

What do you mean? I don't smell anything!

I am one long, fine-looking animal.

Pooh and I have the same favorite food.

What Is a Mustelid?

A mustelid *(MUHS tuh lid)* is a type of mammal. Another name for the mustelid family is the weasel family. Members of this family include badgers, ermines *(UR muhnz)*, ferrets, fishers, grisons *(GRY suhnz)*, minks, otters, polecats, ratels *(RAY tuhls)*, sables, skunks, weasels, and wolverines.

Nearly all mustelids have glands near their rump that make a smelly liquid that is sometimes called musk. And most members of this family have a long, slim body and short legs. This body shape allows mustelids to follow their prey into small holes and narrow cracks.

Mustelids come in many sizes. The largest weasel relatives are sea otters, giant otters, and wolverines. Sea otters may weigh up to 85 pounds (39 kilograms); giant otters can reach 75 pounds (34 kilograms); and wolverines can grow up to 55 pounds (25 kilograms). By contrast, the smallest weasel relative is the least weasel—it weighs about 2 ounces (57 grams).

weasel

badger

otter

ferret

skunk

wolverine

Where in the World Do Badgers and Other Mustelids Live?

Badgers can be found in Asia, Europe, and North America.

American badgers live in southwestern Canada, in the United States from the West Coast to the Midwest, and south to central Mexico. They make their homes mostly in dry country or grasslands with few trees.

Old World badgers live throughout Europe and in northern Asia. Old World badgers prefer to live in forested areas.

Ferret badgers, hog badgers, and stink badgers live in the mountains and forests of southeastern Asia. And, although not a true badger, a similar mustelid that is known as the ratel, or honey badger, can be found in Africa.

World Map

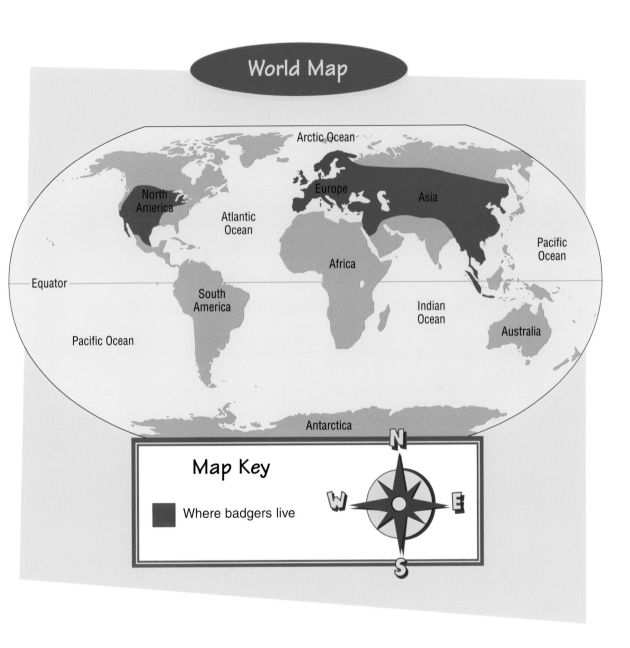

Arctic Ocean

North America

Atlantic Ocean

Europe

Asia

Pacific Ocean

Africa

Equator

South America

Indian Ocean

Pacific Ocean

Australia

Antarctica

Map Key

Where badgers live

N

W   E

S

9

How Can You Tell It's a Badger?

A badger has a short, broad body and a short, bushy tail. It has long claws on its feet. Badgers generally have white and black markings on their head and face.

The American badger has gray or reddish fur and a white stripe running up from its nose. The Old World badger is usually gray on its back, but its underside and legs are black. It has a white face with two dark stripes that run up each side of its face, over its eyes.

American badger

What Is Special About a Badger's Body?

Most badgers have a strong, stout body with short legs. Their front legs are especially strong. Their front paws are equipped with long, sharp claws for digging. Badgers need these digging tools because they often dig for their meals. Badgers also live underground and dig large burrows and tunnels.

Badgers have small eyes and ears. Their hearing is good. Their sense of smell is excellent compared to their other senses, but their eyesight is weak.

All badgers have glands near their rumps that produce a strong-smelling liquid called musk. Some types of badgers squirt out musk to drive away attackers. Badgers also use musk to mark their territory or to mark a scent trail to a source of food or other important places. That way they can find their way around using mainly their noses.

A badger's front paw

How Does a Badger Defend Itself?

Badgers, like most animals, will first try to get away when attacked. They cannot run fast, but they can dig their way to safety at a surprising speed.

They may also try to frighten an attacker by fluffing up their own fur, hissing or growling, and baring their teeth.

All badgers make smelly musk that may be released to defend against an attacker, but stink badgers can squirt their musk at an attacker. If an animal attacks one of these badgers and gets blasted with burning, stinking musk, that animal will think twice before it attacks a stink badger again.

If none of these actions drives off the attacker, badgers can fight back with their strong jaws and powerful teeth. They can give an attacker a nasty bite. Badgers also have tough, loose skin. Because the skin is so loose, the badger can twist around and bite the attacker, even if the attacker has the badger's skin in a tight hold by the teeth.

American badger

Are Badgers Meat-eaters?

Badgers are included in a group named carnivores *(KAHR nuh vawrz)*, which means "meat-eaters." But, badgers and many other animals in this group are actually omnivores *(OM nuh vawrz)*, or animals that eat both meat and plants.

One of the Old World badger's favorite meals is a fat, wriggly earthworm. Why? One reason is that earthworms come to the surface at night, when badgers are out hunting for food. An earthworm in the grass is easy for a badger to gobble up, much easier than digging for rodents. On a damp night, earthworms are plentiful, and a badger can eat its fill with very little effort. Earthworms are also a great source of nutrients.

American badger
eating

In What Kind of Home Does a Badger Live?

All species of badgers live underground, in burrows. But not all badger burrows are alike. Ferret badgers, hog badgers, and stink badgers dig simple burrows. These burrows have one chamber that is large enough for a badger to sleep in or to allow for a mother badger to give birth and care for her young.

The burrows of American badgers may have a few side tunnels branching off the main tunnel. American badgers also may dig several separate burrows in different parts of their large territory. They move from one burrow to another.

Old World badgers, however, dig the most amazing burrows, called setts. Setts can spread over many acres, and may have over 80 entrances. Most setts, however, have about 10 entrances.

American badger looking out from burrow

How Does a Badger Dig?

Badgers carefully choose the place for their burrows. They like to dig their burrows on the side of a slope. This helps water drain away and keeps the burrow dry. The largest burrows are dug in places with soft soil where it is easy to dig. Often, badgers simply enlarge old burrows by digging new tunnels that connect with old ones. They'll also enlarge the abandoned burrows of other animals, such as rabbits.

The badger uses its strong claws to break up the earth. When it has broken up a small pile of dirt, the badger scoots backward out of the tunnel, pushing the soil with its back legs as it goes. Then it kicks this loose soil into a pile outside of the burrow. Badgers can even push, drag, or carry heavy rocks out of the tunnel.

American badger
digging a burrow

What Is It Like Inside a Sett?

The setts of Old World badgers are like underground apartment complexes. These setts are made up of lots of connected tunnels. The tunnels provide a way for badgers to travel safely underground. Wider areas within the tunnels, called chambers, provide places where badgers can sleep, give birth, and raise their young. Badgers drag dried grass, moss, leaves, or ferns into the chambers to make cozy beds. Year after year, badgers add new chambers and tunnels to their setts. In Europe, some badger setts are more than 100 years old.

Badgers keep their setts clean. They relieve themselves in areas outside of the sett. And, every once in a while, the badgers drag their bedding out of the chambers and let it air out in the sun. In addition to their underground homes, Old World badgers occasionally create aboveground nests. These areas are often located near sources of food. They are full of nesting material and are used as temporary resting places.

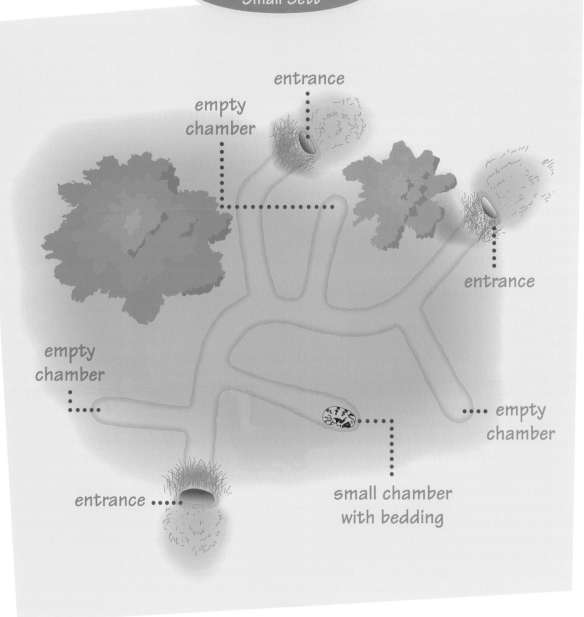

Diagram of a
Small Sett

entrance

empty
chamber

empty
chamber

entrance

entrance

empty
chamber

small chamber
with bedding

23

What Goes On in Old World Badger Families?

Old World badgers live together in a group called a clan. Clans are usually made up of about 10 animals, including adults and young. Each clan usually has a few adult males, or boars, a few adult females, or sows, and a few young, called cubs. When the young males are mature, they usually leave to join other clans. Young females usually stay with their birth clans.

Old World badgers use the scent from their musk glands to recognize each other. Each badger's musk smells a bit different. When all the badgers in a clan put their musk on one another, their scents get mixed together. As a result, each clan has its own unique scent. Each clan member bears the scent of the clan as well as its own scent. That is how Old World badgers recognize members of their own clan.

Old World badger family foraging at night

How Do Baby Badgers Grow?

American and Old World badger cubs are born in the late winter or spring. They are usually born in litters of two or three. They are blind and covered with a thin coat of silvery fur. The mother badger nurses her babies—that is, she feeds them with milk from her body—for the first several weeks of their life. The cubs open their eyes after about a month.

As her cubs grow, an Old World badger mother starts to feed them by bringing up chewed food from her stomach for them to eat. An American badger mother, on the other hand, will bring back dead prey for her young to eat.

Soon, the cubs are ready to leave their home. At first they stay near the entrance. Then they start to explore farther from the burrow or sett, learning how to find food.

By the time Old World badgers are about 4 months old, they can take care of themselves. American badgers do not live in clans, and the young leave their mother after they are about 2 months old.

Three badger cubs

27

What Is the "Partnership" Between Coyotes and American Badgers?

Throughout Canada, the United States, and Mexico, people have observed an odd relationship between badgers and coyotes.

Both coyotes and badgers eat small burrowing animals, such as ground squirrels and prairie dogs. The coyote can chase the squirrels and catch them if they are running around aboveground. The badger, on the other hand, is not fast enough to catch a running ground squirrel. If the ground squirrel is hiding in its burrow, however, it may be safe from the coyote—but not from the badger. The badger can easily dig into a ground squirrel burrow.

A coyote sometimes will watch a badger as it digs for prey. While the badger digs, the prey may run out of its burrow as it tries to escape. Once out in the open, the prey becomes an easy meal for the coyote. Coyotes and badgers do not hunt together in the cooperative sense, but coyotes do benefit from the activities of badgers.

Badger with coyotes

29

Why Are Mustelids So Smelly?

Most mustelids produce smelly musk. They use it mainly to mark their territory. Badgers, for example, mark their food-finding routes with musk so they can find their way around easily. Wolverines mark stashes of food with their musk so other animals will not want to eat it.

Mustelids also use musk for self-defense. The smell of skunks' and stink badgers' musk is really strong. These animals can spray their musk a distance of several feet. For example, when a striped skunk is being attacked, it gives plenty of warning before it sprays. It stamps its feet and raises its fur and tail. Then it bends its body so that its face and rump are both facing its enemy. If the enemy is not scared by this display, the striped skunk sprays a stream of musk. The bad smell can travel for more than a mile. If the musk gets into another animal's eyes, it causes burning pain. If breathed in, it can make a predator sick.

Striped skunk

How Do Mustelids Have Fun?

Many mustelids are playful, especially when they are young. Play is important to animals that hunt for their food. It helps them learn such skills as tracking and catching prey.

Otters and badgers get the prize for being the most playful members of the family. River otters wrestle and romp together. They splash around in the water and chase one another. Otters love to slide. In the summer, they slide down mudbanks on their bellies. In the winter, they slide down snowbanks and scurry through snow tunnels.

Badgers are very playful, too, especially the cubs. They seem to enjoy games of chase and play-fighting, with much nipping, growling, and tumbling around. They also have been seen playing the badger version of king-of-the-hill. In king-of-the-hill, one badger stands on a log or small mound of earth and another tries to knock it off. They also play with objects, such as cans and other human-made objects, that they may find.

European river otters at play

What Are the Enemies of These Animals?

Badgers and their relatives hunt and feed on all sorts of small animals, including rattlesnakes. But some kinds of animals happily eat mustelids for dinner. So mustelids have to be on the lookout for bobcats, bears, wolves, foxes, cougars, and birds of prey, such as hawks and eagles.

Badger relatives that are active at night, such as skunks, weasels, and martens, are hunted by owls. Eagles and hawks kill ferrets, weasels, minks, and the babies of badgers and all their relatives.

White sharks sometimes attack and kill sea otters. But otters do not seem to be the sharks' favorite food. Scientists believe that white sharks bite otters and then let them go. Otters' lean, furry bodies do not have the filling fat that the sharks like to eat.

Badger confronting
a rattlesnake

 35

Which Mustelid Floats Around on Its Back?

Sea otters live in the North Pacific Ocean, off the west coast of North America and the east coast of Siberia. These animals float around on their back, using their webbed back feet to paddle about in the sea. When napping, sea otters often wrap themselves in kelp (a kind of seaweed) to prevent drifting during their sleep. When hungry, they dive to the ocean floor to get their food. They can stay underwater for up to four minutes.

Sea otters spend almost their whole life at sea. They come ashore only rarely, to rest on rocks. They eat, sleep, and raise their young in the water.

Keeping warm is important for mammals that live in the ocean. Other mammals that live in the ocean, such as seals, whales, and dolphins, have a layer of fat, called blubber, under their skin. Blubber keeps these animals warm and helps them stay afloat. Otters do not have blubber, but their thick fur holds a lot of air. This layer of air acts like blubber to help otters stay afloat and keep warm.

Sea otter

Why Does a Sea Otter Carry a Rock?

Sea otters eat seafood. Their diet includes fish, octopuses, and squids. But they also eat a lot of shellfish, including abalones, clams, crabs, sea snails, and mussels. Sea otters grab shellfish with their front paws rather than with their mouths.

To open the hard shell of a shellfish, a sea otter places a rock on its own chest. The sea otter then uses its paws to pound the shellfish on the rock. When the shell breaks open, the sea otter can eat the soft body of the shellfish. A sea otter also uses its large, flat back teeth to crush hard shells.

Sea otter with a
rock for shellfish

Which of These Animals Can Climb Trees?

Many mustelids are good climbers. Spotted skunks sometimes live in hollow trees. Wolverines are known to stash food in trees. Even badgers can climb trees.

But the best tree climbers in this group of animals are the pine martens. These mustelids live in the pine forests of northern Europe and North America. They leap and scamper high in the tree branches, where they capture their favorite prey animals— sleeping squirrels.

The fisher is another member of the weasel family that is quite at home in the treetops. Of the animals the fisher preys upon, there is one that few others will attempt to hunt—the porcupine. The body of a porcupine is covered with sharp spines, called quills, which can cause painful wounds to attackers. But fishers are quick enough to avoid the quills. A fisher usually attacks a porcupine on the ground. But if it needs to get a better angle on its prey, a fisher may climb up a tree and jump down on a porcupine.

40

Two pine martens in a tree

How Do These Animals Spend the Winter?

Most mustelids are quite active all year around. In winter, ermines have been seen scurrying around in snow tunnels. Otters fish under the ice, sometimes swimming long distances before they come up for air through a break in the ice.

Wolverines have large, flat, wide paws that help them walk on top of snow. They are able to hunt large animals, such as deer and sheep, in the winter, because wolverines can move faster in the snow than can the larger animals. Wolverines store food for the winter by stashing it in trees or burying it under the snow or earth.

American badgers often spend most of the winter resting. In winter, food is harder to find. So in the summer and fall, badgers eat as much as they can. This helps their bodies store fat to get ready for winter. In winter, badgers may sleep in their burrows for days or weeks at a time. They can live off fat stored in their body. Skunks that live where the winters are very cold also spend most of the winter in their burrows.

Wolverine in snow

43

Which Mustelid Changes Color in the Winter?

Weasels that live in places with cold, snowy winters get a new "suit of clothes" every winter. These include the ermine (also called the short-tailed weasel), the least weasel, and the long-tailed weasel.

During the summer these weasels' fur is brown. But in winter, when the land is blanketed in white, the weasels turn white, too. Their white fur blends in with the snow and makes it hard for enemies to spot them.

How does the fur turn white? Certain substances produced in these weasels' skin cells give their fur its brown color. These substances are made only in the summer. As summer draws to a close, the skin stops making these chemicals. In the fall, as the brown fur is shed, it is replaced by new white fur.

An ermine in its winter phase

Whose Favorite Food Is Honey?

Ratels are members of the weasel family. Ratels live mainly in eastern and southern Africa. They are often called honey badgers because they resemble badgers and they love to eat honey.

Ratels can climb trees to reach beehives. Their sharp claws make it easy for them to break open a hive. Their tough skin protects them from bee stings. Then they can feast on the honey as well as the bees.

A ratel often finds a beehive with help from a bird called the honey guide. Honey guides eat the honey, bees, and beeswax found in beehives, but they can have trouble getting inside the hive. So, if a honey guide sees a ratel in the area, it gives out a special call that leads the ratel to the hive. When the ratel arrives, it tears open the hive and the two animals feed. Besides honey, ratels also eat small animals, including mammals, birds, reptiles, and insects, as well as some types of plants.

Ratel

Which Weasel Relative Is the Strongest?

Many stories are told about the wolverine's strength, intelligence, and fearlessness. Trappers tell stories of wolverines that figured out how to spring traps and steal the animals caught in them. Wolverines have also been accused of breaking into cabins and stealing food. Many of these stories, however, are probably exaggerated.

It is no exaggeration that the wolverine is the strongest animal of its size. It has a heavy body with powerful limbs. According to some estimates, if a wolverine were the size of a bear, it would be the strongest creature on Earth. The wolverine is a good climber and swimmer, but it spends most of its time on the ground.

Wolverines used to be widespread. But today these animals are quite rare. The southern boundary of their range has been pushed far to the north, and today they live only in far northern North America, north Asia, northern Europe, and in some parts of the western United States.

Wolverine

Why Is the Wolverine Also Called the Glutton?

Glutton is a word for a person who eats too much. Another common name for the wolverine is the glutton, because this animal can eat a lot of food at one time. Wolverines often live in far northern areas. In winter, food can be hard to find. So when food is available, a wolverine gobbles down as much as it can. Wolverines can kill large animals, such as reindeer, moose, or wild sheep. But they mostly eat carrion, small animals, birds and eggs, and berries.

Wolverines have strong jaws and sharp teeth. They can easily crush bones and chew frozen meat. People have reported that wolverines can bite through tin cans. They are strong enough to drag a load of meat three times their own weight.

Wolverines can steal prey from much larger animals, such as mountain lions, wolves, and bears. They scare off these animals by raising their tails, fluffing up their fur, and growling.

Wolverine feeding

Which Ferret Is a Mustelid?

The black-footed ferret is the only wild mustelid that is called a ferret. In the past, black-footed ferrets were common on the Great Plains of North America. Today, they are endangered. The main reason they have disappeared is that their lives depend almost completely on prairie dogs.

Prairie dogs are medium-sized rodents that live in large networks of burrows called prairie dog towns, or colonies. Nearly all of the black-footed ferret's diet is made up of prairie dogs. Ferrets hunt by night. They slip into prairie dog burrows and kill their prey when they are asleep.

Since the 1800's, people have destroyed most prairie dog towns. They did this because farmers and ranchers see prairie dogs as pests. Prairie dogs can eat a lot of the vegetation (plants) that grow on a piece of land. And, if a livestock animal steps into a prairie dog hole, it can break its leg. When the prairie dogs began to disappear, however, so did the black-footed ferrets.

Black-footed ferret

53

Which Member of This Family Is Extinct?

As with many animal families, some mustelids that lived long ago have become extinct. Most extinctions occurred naturally. Not too long ago, however, humans were responsible for the extinction of a large mink with beautiful, reddish-brown fur. This was the sea mink.

Sea minks lived among the rocks along the American coastline eating mainly fish and shellfish. Because their pelt, or fur coat, was so large and valuable, people hunted them until none were left. The last sea mink was seen in the late 1800's.

Sea minks reportedly were almost 3 feet (1 meter) long, including the tail. That is larger than the American mink, a closely related mustelid that lives today. American minks are also prized for their fur. Many are raised in captivity on mink ranches in various parts of the world.

American mink

How Do Mustelids Help People?

Most members of the weasel family are helpful to people because these animals kill and eat harmful rodents, such as mice and rats. Some members of the weasel family are very active. This means that they need a lot of food, so they kill a lot of rodents.

In some parts of the world, tame mustelids are put to work. For example, fishermen in Southeast Asia have trained small-clawed otters to catch fish for them. People have raised ferrets since the 300's B.C. to control rodents. Scientists believe that tame ferrets are descendants of a wild mustelid known as the European polecat. Today, ferrets are common household pets. They are friendly, playful, and can be taught to use a litter box, like cats.

There are, however, some states in which it is illegal to keep a pet ferret. In these areas, lawmakers fear that pet ferrets will bite or attack humans, although owners of pet ferrets deny that this is likely. And, in some regions the fear is that pet ferrets will escape from captivity, form colonies, and threaten native wildlife.

Domestic ferret

Why Do Some People Dislike Mustelids?

Some people dislike mustelids because they sometimes kill animals that are useful to people. For example, weasels break into chicken coops and kill chickens. Weasels sometimes kill more chickens than they can eat.

Wolverines are known to raid people's reindeer herds in Scandinavia. Fur trappers also believe wolverines kill valuable fur-bearing animals. As a result, many wolverines have been killed as pests. Sometimes, people kill otters because they believe they eat too many shellfish. Some workers at fish farms kill otters to keep them from stealing fish.

Badgers' burrows sometimes cause problems for ranchers. Horses and cattle can injure their legs by stepping in a badger's burrow. And, of course, no one wants to be sprayed by a skunk.

European otter
with fish

Are Mustelids in Danger?

Several members of the weasel family are endangered. Sea otters, giant otters, and several other species of otter are endangered. For hundreds of years, people have hunted otters for their thick, beautiful fur. Water pollution affects all otters, and oil spills have killed sea otters. River otters have also suffered because people have built towns and cities along the rivers where the otters live.

The black-footed ferret is one of the world's most endangered animals. In 1987, only 18 known black-footed ferrets were left. The United States government captured them and began a breeding program to save them from extinction. Since then, the government has reintroduced the animals in several states. South Dakota now has at least 200 black-footed ferrets, but the species in the wild is far from recovered.

Giant otter from
South America

Mustelid Fun Facts

→ Scientists observed one female badger in Minnesota that had 50 burrows in her territory. In summer, she never slept in the same burrow two days in a row.

→ River otters can run at speeds of up to 18 miles (29 kilometers) per hour.

→ Sea otters have the thickest fur of all animals. They have about 650,000 hairs per square inch (6.45 square centimeters). The human scalp may have only about 100,000 hairs.

→ The markings on the faces of skunks and badgers are not there to make them look cute. They probably serve as a warning to other animals that they may get squirted by smelly musk if they do not stay away.

→ Female sea otters sometimes adopt orphaned pups and raise them as their own.

→ Other types of animals, such as rabbits and foxes, make their homes in badger setts (or in parts of setts that are not at that time being used by badgers).

Glossary

boar A male badger.

burrow A hole dug in the ground by an animal for refuge or shelter.

carnivore An animal that eats meat.

carrion The flesh of dead animals that is eaten by other animals.

chamber A place in a sett or burrow where animals sleep, give birth, and raise young.

clan A group of Old World badgers living together.

colony A large group of burrows belonging to prairie dogs, also called a prairie dog town.

extinct A species whose members have died out.

gland An organ in an animal's body that makes a special substance, such as musk.

musk A strong-smelling liquid produced by mustelids to drive away attackers and mark territory.

mustelid An animal belonging to the scientific family Mustelidae, which includes badgers, ferrets, otters, skunks, and weasels.

nutrient A substance in food that helps a living thing grow and live.

omnivore An animal that eats both animals and plants.

pelt The skin of a fur-bearing animal that is used to make clothing.

prey An animal that is caught for food by another animal.

quills Sharp spines on porcupines that can cause painful wounds.

rodent A type of animal whose front teeth never stop growing—including beavers, mice, porcupines, and rats.

sett A vast system of burrows that is dug by Old World badgers.

sow A female badger.

territory An area in which an animal lives and which it defends from many other animals.

Index

For more information about Badgers and Other Mustelids, try these resources:

Badgers, by John Darbyshire and Laurie Campbell, Colin Baxter Photography, 1998.

Sea Otters, by Glenn VanBlaricom, Voyageur Press, 2001.

Wonders of Badgers, by Sigmund A. Lavine, Putnam, 1985.

http://animaldiversity.ummz.umich.edu/site/accounts/information/Mustelidae.html

http://www.animalomnibus.com/weasel.htm

http://www.badgers.org.uk/

http://www.honeybadger.com

Badger Classification

Scientists classify animals by placing them into groups. The animal kingdom is a group that contains all the world's animals. Phylum, class, order, and family are smaller groups. Each phylum contains many classes. A class contains orders, an order contains families, and a family contains individual species. Each species also has its own scientific name. (The abbreviation "spp." after a genus name indicates that a group of species from a genus is being discussed.) Here is how the animals in this book fit into this system.

Animals with backbones and their relatives (Phylum Chordata)
Mammals (Class Mammalia)
Carnivores (Order Carnivora)

Badgers and Their Relatives (Family Mustelidae)

Badgers (Subfamily Taxidiinae)
American badger . . . . *Taxidea taxus*

Honey badger (Subfamily Mellivorinae)
Ratel, or honey badger . . . . *Mellivora capensis*

Old World badgers (Subfamily Melinae)
Ferret badgers . . . . *Melogale* spp.
Hog badger . . . . *Arctonyx collaris*
Old World, or Eurasian, badger . . . . *Meles meles*
Stink badgers . . . . *Mydaus* spp.

Otters (Subfamily Lutrinae)
American river otters . . . . *Lontra* spp.
Asian small-clawed otter . . . . *Amblonyx cinereus*
Giant otter . . . . *Pteronura brasiliensis*
Old World, or European, river otter . . . . *Lutra lutra*
Sea otter . . . . *Enhydra lutris*

Skunks (Subfamily Mephitinae)
Spotted skunk . . . . *Spilogale* spp.
Striped skunk . . . . *Mephitis mephitis*

Wolverines, martens, weasels, minks (Subfamily Mustelinae)
American mink . . . . *Mustela vison*
Black-footed ferret . . . . *Mustela nigripes*
Ermine, or short-tailed weasel . . . . *Mustela erminea*
European polecat . . . . *Mustela putorius*
Domestic ferret . . . . *Mustela putorius furo*
Least weasel . . . . *Mustela nivalis*
Long-tailed weasel . . . . *Mustela frenata*
Sea mink . . . . *Mustela macrodon*
American pine marten . . . . *Martes americana*
European pine marten . . . . *Martes martes*
Fisher . . . . *Martes pennanti*
Sable . . . . *Martes zibellina*
Wolverine . . . . *Gulo gulo*

Animals

Written by Jinny Johnson
Illustrated by Mike Atkinson

This is a Parragon Publishing Book
This edition published in 2002

Parragon Publishing
Queen Street House
4 Queen Street
Bath BA1 1HE, UK

ISBN: 0-75259-654-3

Printed in China

Produced by Miles Kelly Publishing Ltd

Cover design: Design Principals

Contents

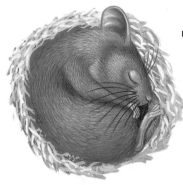

Dormouse

The dormouse normally weighs up to 1 oz (25 g), but it puts on extra fat before it hibernates.

Do dormice really sleep a lot?

Dormice do sleep through the winter. This hibernation may start in October and last until April, longer in cold climates. The dormouse sleeps in in a cozy nest on the ground or in a burrow.

Where do porcupines live?

There are two groups of porcupines. New World porcupines live in North and South America and live in trees. Old World porcupines live in Africa and parts of Asia. They are ground-dwelling animals. All porcupines are covered in long sharp spines, which look fearsome and help protect them from their enemies.

Porcupine

If attacked, the porcupine runs backward toward its enemy, driving in its sharp spines.

Why do beavers build dams?

BEAVERS BUILD THEIR HOMES—OR LODGES—IN STREAMS OR RIVERS But first they need to build a dam to make an area of still water, or the current would wash the lodge away. With their huge front teeth, the beavers cut down trees to build the dam. They plaster the sides with mud and fill gaps with stones and sticks. The lodge is built of sticks behind the dam and has an underwater entrance. The beavers sleep, store food, and care for their young in the lodge. They have to keep repairing both the dam and the lodge with more sticks and mud. Beavers live in North America and in parts of Europe and Asia.

Which is the smallest rodent?

One of the smallest rodents is the pygmy mouse of North America. This is only about 4 in (10 cm) long, including its tail, and weighs ¼ oz (7 g). The harvest mouse of Europe and Asia is only slightly bigger.

What do beavers eat?

Beavers eat plant food. In spring and summer they feed on fresh green leaves and grasses. In autumn they gather woody stems to eat. Some of these are stored under water near the lodge to keep fresh for the winter months.

How many kinds of rodent are there?
There are more than 1,600 different species of rodent, including squirrels, hamsters, and beavers as well as rats and mice. Rodents live all over the world in every kind of habitat from the icy Arctic to scorching deserts and humid rain forests.

Can flying squirrels really fly?
No, but they can glide some distance from tree to tree. When the flying squirrel leaps into the air, it stretches out the skin flaps at the sides of its body. These act like a parachute, enabling it to glide gently down from one branch to another.

Is a guinea pig a rodent?
A guinea pig is a rodent. Wild guinea pigs, also known as cavies, live in South America, where they feed on leaves and grasses. Most cavies are about 9 in (22 cm) long, but one type, the long-legged, harelike mara, is up to 30 in (75 cm) long.

Why do rodents get long in the tooth?
The two sharp teeth at the front of the rodent's jaw—called incisors— are the ones it uses for gnawing. A rodent's incisors get worn down as it gnaws tough food, but they keep on growing throughout its life.

Which is the biggest rodent?
The largest rodent in the world is the capybara, which lives in South America. It measures up to 53 in (1.3 meters) long and weighs up to 140 lb (64 kg). Capybaras live by water and feed on grasses.

How big is a beaver?
A fully grown beaver measures up to 67 in (1.7 meters) long, including its long flat tail. It weighs as much as 60 lb (27 kg) and is the second heaviest rodent in the world.

A beaver lodge

The beaver swims with the help of its webbed back feet and its large flattened tail.

When is a dog really a rat?

A PRAIRIE DOG IS ACTUALLY NOT A DOG AT ALL. IN FACT IT'S A TYPE OF RODENT, and lives in North America. Each prairie dog family, called a coterie, makes a burrow of connecting chambers and tunnels. A coterie contains one adult male and up to four females and their young. Groups of coteries live near each other in huge areas of burrows called towns. Prairie dogs feed mostly on grasses and other plants. While the family is feeding, one prairie dog keeps watch. It barks loudly to warn the others of any danger.

The living chamber in the beaver's lodge is above the water level.

How many kinds of bear are there?

THERE ARE EIGHT SPECIES OF BEAR. THEY RANGE IN SIZE FROM THE SUN BEAR, which weighs only about 60 lb (27 kg), to huge polar bears and brown bears. The brown bear is the most widespread bear. It lives in northern North America and parts of Europe and Asia. In North America the brown bear is sometimes called the grizzly. Brown bears have a varied diet. They eat grasses, roots, and berries, but they also catch insects, fish, and other larger animals, as well as scavenging the carcasses of dead creatures such as deer and seals.

The panda's front paws have a special extra digit to help it grip bamboo stems.

Which is the biggest bear?
The polar bear, which lives in the Arctic. Fully grown males are up to 8.5 ft (2.6 meters) long. Polar bears have thick white fur to keep them warm in their icy home. They hunt seals and occasionally also young walrus and birds.

Is the giant panda a bear?
For many years experts argued about whether this animal should be grouped with bears or raccoons or classed in a separate family of its own. Genetic evidence now suggests that the panda is a member of the bear family.

What do giant pandas eat?
The main food of the giant panda is bamboo. An adult panda eats up to 33 lb (15 kg) of bamboo leaves and stems a day. Pandas also eat a small amount of other plants and even some little animals.

How many kinds of wild dog are there?
There are about 35 species in the dog family, including foxes, wolves, coyotes, and hunting dogs. Wild dogs live all over the world, except in New Zealand, New Guinea, and a few other islands. All are good runners and hunt other animals to eat.

A red fox is up to 25 in (63 cm) long, with a bushy tail of up to 16 in (40 cm). Foxes live and hunt in an area called a territory, which they mark with their scent.

Where do giant pandas live?
Giant pandas live in bamboo forests in the mountains of central China. Most of these forests have now been made into special reserves to try and protect the rare pandas. Some pandas also live in captivity in zoos in China and other countries.

Red fox

What do foxes eat?
Foxes, such as the red fox, are hunting animals. They kill and eat small creatures, including rats, mice, and rabbits. But foxes are very adaptable—they will eat more or less anything that comes their way, such as birds and birds' eggs, insects, and even fruit and berries. And more and more foxes in cities are feasting on our discarded food from rubbish bins and compost heaps.

How big is a wolf pack?

In areas where there are plenty of large animals to catch, a pack may contain up to 20 wolves. Hunting in a pack means that the wolves can kill prey much larger than themselves, such as moose. A wolf pack has a home range, or territory, which it defends against other wolves.

How do wolf cubs learn how to hunt?

Wolf cubs learn how to hunt by watching their parents and other pack members and by playing. As the cubs run around and pounce on one another, they are also learning how to attack and ambush prey.

Can polar bears swim?

Polar bears can swim well and spend long periods in the freezing Arctic water. They are well equipped to survive the cold. A polar bear has a dense layer of underfur as well as a heavy, glossy outer coat. Under the skin is a thick layer of fat to give further protection.

Are there bears in the jungle?

Yes, there are two kinds of bear that live in jungle, or rain forest. Some spectacled bears live in South American rain forest, and the sun bear lives in rain forest in parts of Southeast Asia.

How big is a baby bear?

Although adult bears are so big they have tiny babies. A huge polar bear, weighing more than several people, gives birth to cubs of only about 28 oz (800 g), far smaller than most human babies. Baby pandas are tinier still. The mother weighs up to 220 lb (100 kg) but her newborn cubs are only 3–5 oz (85–140 g).

What is a dingo?

Dingoes are wild dogs that live in Australia. They are descended from dogs domesticated more than 3,500 years ago by the earliest aboriginal inhabitants. They live in family groups and hunt sheep and rabbits. A fence 3,307 miles (5,322 km) long has been built across southeastern Australia to try to keep dingoes out of important sheep-grazing lands.

Brown bear

A male brown bear stands up to 84 in (213 cm) tall and weighs up to 838 lb (380 kg). Bears like plant food and will reach up into trees to pick juicy fruit or berries.

Do bears sleep through the winter?

BROWN BEARS AND AMERICAN AND ASIAN BLACK BEARS THAT LIVE IN THE far north do sleep for much of the winter. Food supplies are poor and the bears hide themselves away in warm dens and live off their own fat reserves. Before their long sleep and fast, the bears eat as much food as they can to build up their body fat. They may not eat or drink again for as long as six months. A bear's body temperature drops only slightly during the winter sleep and it wakes easily if disturbed. Female bears may give birth to a litter of cubs during this time.

Meerkats on guard

Meerkats thrive in the hostile Kalahari desert by working as a team. A group of adults watch out for predators while others are out hunting.

What is a meerkat?

A meerkat is a type of mongoose, which lives in Africa. Meerkats form large groups of up to 30 or more animals, which share the guarding of young and finding of food. Sentry meerkats often stand up on their hind legs to watch out for danger.

Which cat runs the fastest?

The cheetah is the fastest running cat and one of the speediest of all animals over short distances. It has been timed running at 60 mph (105 kph) over 110 yds (100 meters). Olympic sprinters can reach only about 30 mph (48 kph).

What is a panther?

A panther is simply a leopard with a black coat instead of spots. It is not a separate species of cat. Leopards live in Africa and Asia.

What does a mongoose eat?

The mongoose is a fast-moving little hunter. It will kill small creatures such as rats, mice, and frogs and will also take anything else it can find, including insects and birds' eggs. A mongoose will even tackle a large snake.

How many kinds of cat are there?

There are about 35 species of wild cat, ranging from the tiger to the African wild cat, which is the main ancestor of domestic cats. Cats live in most parts of the world in every sort of habitat from tropical rainforest and desert to the icy lands of Siberia. There are no wild cats in Antarctica, Australia, or New Zealand.

The pattern of stripes on a tiger's skin is unique. No two tigers have quite the same pattern.

Tiger

Which big cat is the biggest?

TIGERS ARE THE BIGGEST OF THE BIG CATS. THEY MEASURE UP TO 10 FT (3 METERS) long, including the tail, and weigh 550 lb (250 kg) or more. Tigers are becoming very rare. They live in parts of Asia, from snowy Siberia in the north to the tropical rain forests of Sumatra. There is only one species of tiger, but those in the north tend to be larger and have thicker, lighter colored fur than their relations farther south. Tigers live alone, coming together only for mating. The female rears her cubs without the help of her mate. At first the cubs stay close to the den, but when they are about six months old they begin to go with their mother on hunts and learn how to find food for themselves.

What do lions do all day?

Like domestic cats, lions are actually asleep for a surprisingly large part of the day. As many as 22 hours a day are spent resting and grooming. The rest of the time is taken up with looking for prey, hunting, and feeding. Lionesses do most of the hunting, but they share the catch with the rest of the pride.

Where do jaguars live?

Jaguars live in the forests of Central and South America. They are the largest South American cats and measure up to 6 ft (1.8 meters) long with a tail of up to 36 in (90 cm). Despite its size, the jaguar is a good climber and often clambers up a tree to watch for prey. It hunts other forest animals such as peccaries and capybaras as well as birds, turtles, and fish.

Why are lions unlike other cats?

MOST CATS LIVE ALONE. LIONS LIVE AND HUNT IN A GROUP CALLED A PRIDE.
Tigers, cheetahs, and other big cats live alone, unless rearing young. A lion pride includes several adult males and a number of females, young lions, and cubs. Living in a group means that there are always some adults to look after the cubs while others are off hunting. And working together, lions can bring down animals much larger than themselves, such as wildebeest and zebra.

What is a snow leopard?

The snow leopard is a big cat that lives in the Himalaya Mountains. It has a beautiful pale coat with dark markings, which has made it the target of fur poachers. Killing snow leopards for their fur is now illegal, but poaching still goes on.

How different are our pet cats from wild cats?

Pet cats and wild cats have exactly the same body structure and skeleton. Both rely heavily on smell for information about the world and they mark their territories by spraying urine or by rubbing the body against trees or other objects. All cats are meat eaters and cannot live on a diet of plant foods.

Is a civet a kind of cat?

No, civets belong to a separate family, which also includes mongooses, meerkats, and genets. Most civets live in tropical forests in Southeast Asia or Africa. They have a long, slender body, short legs and a long tail. The African civet is about 37 in (95 cm) long with a tail of about 20 in (50 cm). It hunts small mammals, birds, reptiles, and insects.

Why do tigers have stripes?

A tiger's stripes help it hide among grasses and leaves so it can surprise its prey. Tigers cannot run fast for long distances so they depend on being able to get close to their prey before making the final pounce. The stripes help to break up their outline and make them hard for prey to see.

9

How long are an elephant's tusks?

An elephant's tusks grow throughout its life, so the oldest elephants have the longest tusks. An old male elephant may have tusks that measure up to 11 ft (3.5 meters) and weigh 264 lb (120 kg).

African elephant

An elephant's tusks are actually very long upper teeth.

How much do elephants eat?

A fully grown elephant eats 220 to 440 lb (100 to 200 kg) of plant food a day, including grass, twigs, branches, leaves, flowers, and fruits.

What do elephants do with their trunks?

THE ELEPHANT'S TRUNK IS VERY USEFUL. WITHOUT IT, AN ELEPHANT could not reach the ground to feed because its neck is so short. The trunk is also used for taking food from high in the trees and for breaking off branches. The elephant can smell with its trunk, pick up tiny objects, and gently caress its young. It drinks by sucking up water into its trunk and squirting it into its mouth. It also sprays water or dust over itself to clean its skin.

The elephant flaps its huge ears to help keep itself cool.

Giraffe

How tall is a giraffe?
A male giraffe stands up to 18 ft (5.5 meters) tall to the tips of its horns. It has an extraordinarily long neck, and front legs that are longer than its back legs so the body slopes down toward the tail. The long neck allows it to feed on leaves high in trees that other animals cannot reach.

The giraffe's tongue can stretch out up to 18 in (46 cm) to help it gather leaves from tall trees.

How many bones are there in a giraffe's neck?
A giraffe has seven bones in its neck, just like other mammals, including humans. But the giraffe's neck bones are much longer than those of other animals, and have more flexible joints between them.

The elephant's gray skin is up to 1½ in (4 cm) thick and has a fine covering of hairs.

What is an okapi?
An okapi is a relative of the giraffe that lives in the African rain forest. It was discovered as recently as 1901 by a British explorer. It has small horns on its head and a long tongue like a giraffe's—but it does not have a long neck.

How can you tell an African elephant from an Asian elephant?

THE AFRICAN ELEPHANT IS BIGGER AND HAS LARGER EARS AND LONGER TUSKS. The head and body of the African elephant measures up to 24.5 ft (7.5 meters) long. The Asian elephant measures up to 21 ft (6.5 meters) and has a more humped back. There is another difference at the end of the long trunk. The African elephant's trunk has two flexible fingerlike lips, while the Asian animal's trunk has only one.

Are rhinoceroses fierce animals?
Despite their ferocious appearance and huge horns, rhinos are peaceful, plant-eating animals. But if threatened, a rhino will charge its enemy, galloping at high speed with its huge head held down ready to attack. Mothers defending their young can be particularly dangerous.

Can hippos swim?
The hippo spends most of its day in or near water and comes out on to land at night to feed on plants. It does not really swim, but it walks or runs along underwater or on the bottom of the river at surprising speeds.

How big is a baby elephant?
A newborn baby elephant weighs up to 264 lb (120 kg) and stands up to 40 in (1 meter) high. It feeds on its mother's milk for at least two years, by which time it may weigh more than 1,322 lb (600 kg), and it may continue suckling for up to six years.

11

Do all marsupials live in Australia?

Most of the 260 or so species of marsupial live in Australia and New Guinea, but there are about 80 species of marsupial opossum in South America. One of these also lives in North America.

Which is the smallest marsupial?

The smallest marsupials are the mouselike ningauis, which live in Australia. These little creatures are only about 2 in (5 cm) long and weigh only a few grams. They feed on insects.

Do all marsupials have a pouch?

Most female marsupials have a pouch, but not all. Some very small marsupials such as the shrew opossums of South America do not have a pouch. Others, such as the American opossums, simply have flaps of skin around the nipples and not a full pouch. The tiny young cling on to the nipples.

Do any marsupials swim?

The water opossum, which lives in South America, is an excellent swimmer and has webbed back feet. Strong muscles keep its pouch closed when the opossum is in water.

Why does a kangaroo have a pouch?

A T BIRTH, KANGAROOS ARE VERY TINY AND EXTREMELY POORLY DEVELOPED. In fact, a kangaroo is only about ³/₄ in (2 cm) long when it is born. The female kangaroo has a pouch so that its young can complete their development in safety. The tiny newborn crawls up to the pouch by itself and starts to suckle on one of the nipples inside the pouch. A young kangaroo, or joey, stays in the pouch until it weighs about 20 lb (9 kg). Pouched animals like kangaroos are called marsupials.

How many kinds of kangaroo and wallaby are there?

There are about 60 different species of kangaroo and wallaby. All live in Australia or New Guinea. The red kangaroo, which weighs about 198 lb (90 kg), is the largest, and the tiny musky rat kangaroo, weighing only 1.2 lb (0.5 kg), is the smallest.

What do kangaroos eat?

Kangaroos eat grass and the leaves of low-growing plants, just like deer and antelopes do in the northern hemisphere.

Red kangaroo

Only the male red kangaroo has a reddish coat. Females are bluish-gray.

What is a Tasmanian devil?
The Tasmanian devil is the largest of the carnivores, or flesh-eating marsupials. It is about 36 in (90 cm) long, including its tail, and has sharp teeth and strong jaws. The devil feeds mostly on carrion—the flesh of animals that are already dead—but it does also kill prey such as sheep and birds.

How much does a koala eat every day?
A koala eats about 1 lb (500 g) of eucalyptus leaves every day, which it chews down to a fine pulp with its broad teeth. The leaves do not provide much energy, but koalas are slow-moving animals and sleep up to 18 hours a day.

Is a platypus a marsupial?
No, the platypus is not a marsupial, but it is an unusual animal and it does live in Australia. Unlike most mammals, which give birth to live young, the platypus lays eggs. The mother leaves her two or three eggs to incubate in a burrow for up to two weeks. When they hatch, the young feed on the milk that flows from openings in the mother's body.

What are bandicoots?
Bandicoots are a group of small marsupials that live in Australia and New Guinea. Most have short legs, a rounded body and a long pointed nose. They have strong claws, which they use to dig worms and other small creatures from the ground.

Koala bear

The koala has strong claws to help it hold on to branches as it climbs in search of food.

Is a koala really a kind of bear?

NO, IT'S A MARSUPIAL LIKE A KANGAROO AND NOT RELATED TO BEARS AT ALL. Koalas live in Australia in eucalyptus forests. They feed almost entirely on eucalyptus leaves, preferring those of only a few species. A baby koala spends its first six or seven months in the pouch and then rides on its mother's back until it is able to fend for itself. A baby weighs less than half a gram at birth, but when fully grown the average koala measures about 30 in (78 cm) long and weighs up to 24 lb (11 kg). Females are much smaller than males.

How fast do kangaroos move?
A kangaroo bounds along on its strong back legs at up to 40 mph (65 kph). It can cover 39 ft (12 meters) in one bound.

What is a wombat?
A wombat is a small bearlike marsupial with a heavy body and short strong legs. It digs burrows to shelter in and feeds mostly on grass. Its pouch opens to the rear so that it does not fill up with earth when the wombat is burrowing.

What do gorillas eat?

Gorillas eat plant food, such as leaves, buds, stems, and fruit. Because their diet is juicy, gorillas rarely need to drink.

Which is the smallest monkey?

The smallest monkey is the pygmy marmoset, which lives in South American rain forest. It is about 15 in (40 cm) long, but half of this is tail, and it weighs only about 5 oz (150 g).

What is an ape?

Apes are the most advanced animals in the primate group, which also includes animals such as lemurs, bush babies, and monkeys. There are three families of apes. One includes all the different kinds of gibbons. The second contains the gorilla, chimpanzee, and orangutan and the third has one species only—humans.

Where do orangutans live?

Orangutans live in Southeast Asia in the rain forests of Sumatra and Borneo. This ape has long reddish fur and spends most of its life in the trees. Fruit is its main food but the orangutan also eats leaves, insects, and even eggs and small animals. The orangutan is active during the day. At night it sleeps on the ground or in a nest of branches in the trees.

Gorillas usually move on all fours, leaning on the knuckles of their front limbs.

Which is the biggest ape?

THE GORILLA—A FULLY GROWN MALE STANDS UP TO 5.5 FT (1.7 METERS) TALL and weighs as much as 400 lb (180 kg). Gorillas live in rain forest in West and Central Africa. A family group contains an adult male, several females and a number of young of different ages. The male, known as a silverback because of the white hair on his back, leads the group.

Gorilla family

Do chimpanzees hunt prey?

Yes they do. Although fruit is the main food of chimpanzees, they also eat insects and hunt young animals such as monkeys. Male chimpanzees usually do the hunting. They work together in a group, some cutting a couple of animals out of the herd and driving them toward other chimps, who will make the kill. The rest of the troop then joins in to share the meat.

Chimpanzee

An adult chimpanzee is up to 33 in (85 cm) long and does not have a tail.

Why does the monkey have a long tail?

TO HELP IT BALANCE AND CONTROL ITS MOVEMENTS AS IT LEAPS FROM branch to branch in the rain forest. The tails of South American monkeys are even more useful than those of their African and Asian relatives, because they are prehensile. A prehensile tail has special muscles that the monkey can use to twine round branches and help it climb—it's almost like having a fifth leg. The naked skin on the underside of the tail is ridged to improve grip.

Chimpanzees climb well and find much of their food in trees.

Do chimpanzees use tools?

Yes. The chimpanzee can get food by poking a stick into an ants' nest. It pulls out the stick and licks off the ants. It also uses stones to crack nuts, and it makes sponges from chewed leaves to mop up water or wipe its body.

Which monkey makes the loudest noise?

Howler monkeys not only shout louder than other monkeys—they are among the noisiest of all animals. Troops of monkeys call to each other and their voices carry for more than 0.6 miles (1 km).

Do any monkeys live in cold places?

Most monkeys are found in warm areas near the equator, but some macaque monkeys live in cooler places. The rhesus macaque lives in the Himalayas as well as in parts of China and India, and the Japanese macaque survives freezing winters with the help of its thick coat.

Where do chimpanzees live?

Chimpanzees live in forest and grasslands in West and Central Africa. There is another less familiar chimpanzee species called the pygmy chimpanzee, or bonobo, which lives in rain forests in Zaire/Congo in Africa. It is slimmer and lighter than the common chimpanzee and spends more of its time in trees.

How many kinds of monkey are there?

About 133 species in three main groups. One group lives in Africa and Asia. The other two groups live in Central and South America.

Do chimpanzees live in family groups?

Yes, in very large families that may include between 25 and 100 animals, led by a dominant male. Each group has its own home range.

Californian sea lion

How can you tell a seal from a sea lion?

WITH PRACTICE! SEALS AND SEA LIONS BOTH HAVE STREAMLINED BODIES adapted to marine living, and flippers instead of limbs. But there are several differences between them. Sea lions have small ear flaps, but seals have only ear openings, no flaps. Sea lions can bring their back flippers under the body to help them move on land. Seals cannot do this—they simply drag themselves along. Sea lions swim by moving their front flippers. Seals swim by moving the back flippers and the rear of the body.

The sea lion tucks its back flippers under itself when on land.

How do seals keep warm in cold sea?
A layer of fatty blubber under the skin helps to keep seals and sea lions warm. The blubber may be up to 4 in (10 cm) thick. These animals also have a covering of fur.

How fast do seals and sea lions swim?
A Californian sea lion has been timed swimming at 25 mph (40 kph). On land the crabeater seal can move at up to 11 mph (19 kph) as it toboggans over ice.

How deep do seals dive?
The Weddell seal, which lives in Antarctic waters, is one of the deepest-diving seals. It can go down to depths of more than 1,640 ft (500 meters) in search of food. When the seal dives, blood flow is cut off to all but essential organs such as the heart.

How big are sea lions?
The biggest, the steller sea lion, is about 90 in (230 cm) long and weighs as much as 2,200 lb (1,000 kg). Females are much smaller and weigh only about 595 lb (270 kg). The smallest is probably the Galapagos fur seal, which weighs only about 140 lb (64 kg).

Are baby seals and sea lions born in water?
No, they are born on land. Seals and sea lions spend most of their lives in water but they do come out on to land to give birth. They remain on land for a number of weeks, feeding their young on their rich milk.

Harp seal

Which is the smallest seal?

The ringed seal is one of the smallest seals. The male grows to about 4.5 ft (1.4 meters) long and weighs up to 198 lb (90 kg), although some are only 110 lb (50 kg). Females are slightly smaller than males. Ringed seals live in Arctic waters and eat fish and shellfish.

How big is a walrus?

The largest male walruses are more than 10 ft (3 meters) long and weigh 2,645 lb (1,200 kg). Females are smaller, averaging 9 ft (2.7 meters) long and weighing about 1,760 lb (800 kg) The walrus's skin is up to 1½ in (4 cm) thick and covered with coarse hairs. The thick skin helps protect the walrus from the tusks of others.

Do seals live in fresh water?

Yes, there is a species of freshwater seal in Lake Baikal in Russia. Baikal is the deepest freshwater lake in the world and holds more water than any other. Thousands of seals live there, feeding on freshwater fish and resting on the remote islands in the middle of the lake.

How long are a walrus's tusks?

The tusks of an adult male walrus can be up to 22 in (55 cm) long. Some people think that a walrus uses its tusks to dig shellfish from the seabed, but other experts believe that the tusks are just for display and attracting mates.

Are any seals very rare?

Yes, monk seals, which live in the Caribbean, Mediterranean, and Hawaiian seas, are extremely rare. The Caribbean seal is probably already extinct. These are the only seals that live in warm seas, closer to human activity than other seals, so they have suffered greater habitat disturbance.

Which is the biggest seal?

The male elephant seal is the biggest of all the seals. It is 5 meters (16 ft) long and weighs 2,400 kg (5,300 lb), nearly as much as an elephant.

How many kinds of seal and sea lion are there?

There are about 14 species of sea lion, 18 species of seal, and one species of walrus. Most sea lions live along North Pacific coasts and on the southern coasts of Africa, Australia and South America. Most seals live in waters to the far north and south of the world, and the walrus lives in Arctic seas.

What do seals and sea lions eat?

FISH IS THEIR MAIN DIET, BUT SOME ALSO EAT SHELLFISH AND CATCH LARGER PREY. Some seals have a more varied diet. The crabeater seal feeds mostly on krill, small shrimplike crustaceans. The bearded seal eats seabed creatures such as clams, and the leopard seal preys on the young of other seals as well as birds and fish.

Do seals and sea lions breathe air?

Seals and sea lions are mammals so they have to come to the surface regularly to breathe air. But they can stay underwater much longer than we can. Dives lasting 20 minutes or more are common and the Weddell seal has been timed making a dive of over 70 minutes.

Fur seals have extra-thick fur and look like true seals. But their small ear flaps show they are really types of sea lion.

Dolphins

How big is a baby blue whale?
A baby blue whale is about 23 ft (7 meters) long at birth and is the biggest baby in the animal kingdom. It weighs about 8 tons—that is more than a fully grown elephant.

Which is the biggest whale?

THE BLUE WHALE IS THE LARGEST WHALE, AND ALSO THE LARGEST MAMMAL THAT has ever lived. It measures more than 100 ft (30 meters) long. It weighs at least 100 tons and the biggest blue whales may weigh more than twice this amount. Although it is so huge, the blue whale is not a fierce hunter. It eats tiny shrimplike creatures called krill. It may gobble up as many as four million of these in a day.

Dolphins leap out of the water as they swim and dive back in head first.

What is a porpoise?
A porpoise is a small whale with a rounded head, not a beaked snout like a dolphin. There are about six species of porpoise, which live in coastal waters in the Atlantic and Pacific. They feed on fish and squid.

Which whale dives deepest?
The sperm whale dives to at least 3,300 ft (1,000 meters) below the surface of the sea and may go down to even greater depths when chasing giant squid to eat.

Do whales ever come to land?
No, whales spend their whole lives in the sea. But they do breathe air and have to come to the surface regularly to take breaths.

Blue whales once lived in all oceans. Now most are found in Antarctic waters.

Blue whale

Is a dolphin
a kind of whale?

A DOLPHIN IS A SMALL WHALE. MOST OF THE 37 OR SO SPECIES OF DOLPHIN live in the sea, but there are five that live in rivers. The biggest dolphin is usually known as the killer whale, or orca, and grows up to 31 ft (9.4 meters) long. Dolphins have a streamlined shape and a beaked snout containing lots of sharp teeth. They are fast swimmers and they catch sea creatures such as fish and squid to eat. A form of ultrasound helps dolphins find their prey. A dolphin gives off a series of high-frequency clicking sounds that bounce off anything in their path. The echoes tell the dolphin about the size and direction of the prey.

Do whales give birth in the water?
Yes, they do. The baby whale comes out of the mother's body tail first so that it does not drown during birth. As soon as the head emerges, the mother and the other females attending the birth help the baby whale swim to the surface to take its first breath.

What is a narwhal?
A narwhal is a whale with a single long tusk at the front of its head. The tusk is actually a tooth, which grows out from the upper jaw. It can be as much as 9 ft (2.7 meters) long. Only male narwhals have tusks and they may use them in battles with other males.

Do humpback whales really sing?
Yes, they do. They make a series of sounds, including high whistles and low rumbles, that may continue for hours. No one knows exactly why the humpback sings, but it may be to court a mate or to keep in touch with others in the group.

Why do some whales migrate?
Whales such as humpbacks migrate—travel from place to place—to find the best conditions for feeding and breeding. They spend much of the year feeding in the waters of the Arctic and Antarctic, where there is lots of krill to eat. When it is time to give birth, the humpbacks travel to warmer waters near the equator.

How fast do whales swim?
Blue whales normally swim at about 5 mph (8 kph) but can move at speeds of up to 18 mph (30 kph) when disturbed. Some small whales, such as pilot whales and dolphins, may swim at more than 30 mph (50 kph).

How does a blue whale feed?
A blue whale filters small shrimplike creatures called krill from the water. Hanging from the whale's upper jaw are lots of plates of a fringed bristly material called baleen. The whale opens its mouth and water, and krill, flows in. The whale forces the water through the baleen with its tongue. The water flows out at the sides of the mouth, leaving the krill behind on the baleen for the whale to swallow.

Puffer fish

This fish puffs up its body when in danger.

How fast do fish swim?
The sailfish is one of the fastest swimming fish. It has been timed moving at speeds of more than 62 mph (100 kph). Marlins and tunas are also fast swimmers. All these fish have sleek streamlined bodies.

Does a stingray sting?
A stingray gets its name from the sharp spine near the base of its tail. This carries poison and causes a nasty wound if the fish drives it into the flesh of its enemy. It can even kill a human.

Are flatfishes born flat?
No, they are not. Young flatfishes have normal bodies with an eye on each side. As they grow, the body flattens and one eye moves, so that both are on the upper surface. The fish lies on the seabed with its eyed side uppermost so it can see.

Are there any poisonous fish?

YES, THERE ARE—AND THE PUFFER FISH IS ONE OF THE MOST POISONOUS OF ALL.
It has a powerful poison in some of its internal organs, such as the heart and liver, which can kill a human. Despite this, puffer fish is a delicacy in Japan, where chefs are specially trained to remove the poisonous parts and prepare the fish. A puffer fish also has another way of defending itself. It can puff its body up with water and air until it is at least twice its normal size. This makes it very hard for any predator to swallow. Some puffer fish are covered with spines that stick up when the body is inflated.

Which is the fiercest freshwater fish?
The piranha, which lives in rivers in tropical Central and South America, is the fiercest of all freshwater fish. Each fish is only about 12 in (30 cm) long, but a shoal of hundreds attacking together can kill and eat a much larger animal in seconds. The piranha's weapons are its extremely sharp triangular-shaped teeth, which it uses to chop flesh from its victim. But not all piranhas are dangerous killers. Some species feed only on plants.

How many kinds of shark are there?
There are about 370 different species of shark living all over the world. They range in size from tiny fish only 10 in (25 cm) long, to the giant whale shark, which can grow to 50 ft (15 meters).

Are electric eels really electric?
Yes, they are. The electric eel's body contains special muscles that can release electrical charges into the water. These are powerful enough to stun and kill its prey.

Why does a flying fish "fly"?
A flying fish usually lifts itself above the water to escape from danger. It has extra large fins, which act as its "wings". After building up speed in the water, the fish lifts its fins and glides above the surface for a short distance.

How big is a great white shark?

Are all sharks killers?
No, two of the largest sharks, the whale shark and the basking shark, eat only tiny shrimplike creatures. They filter these from the water through special sievelike structures in the mouth.

GREAT WHITE SHARKS ARE MOSTLY ABOUT 23 FT (7 METERS) LONG, but some can grow up to 40 ft (12 meters). They live in warm seas all over the world. Great white sharks are fierce hunters and attack large fish and other creatures such as sea lions and porpoises. Their main weapons are their large, jagged-edged teeth, which they use to kill prey and to tear it apart. Behind these teeth are rows of new ones, ready to replace teeth at the front that get damaged or broken.

Great white shark

The shark's teeth may be up to 3 in (7.5 cm) long.

A shark may swim at speeds of up to 25 mph (40 kph) for short periods.

Poison-arrow frog

The poison-arrow frog is one of the most poisonous of all animals.

Do all frogs lay their eggs in water?
No, some frogs have very unusual breeding habits. The male marsupial frog, for example, carries his mate's eggs on his back. A layer of skin grows over them to protect them. The male Darwin's frog keeps his mate's eggs in his mouth until they have developed into tiny frogs.

What do frogs eat?
Adult frogs catch insects and spiders and other small creatures such as crayfish and even other frogs to eat. Tadpoles usually feed on small water plants.

What is an amphibian?
An amphibian is a creature that lives in water and on land. Amphibians evolved from fish and were the first vertebrates (creatures with backbones) to live on land. There are about 3,000 species of amphibian, including frogs, toads, newts, and salamanders.

What is a tadpole?
A tadpole is the young, or larva, of an amphibian such as a frog or newt. The amphibian egg is usually laid in water and hatches out into a small, swimming creature with a long tail called a tadpole. The tadpole feeds on water plants and gradually develops into its adult form.

Why do frogs croak?
Male frogs make their croaking calls to attract females. The frog has a special sac of skin under its chin, which blows up and helps make the call louder.

Which is the smallest frog?
The smallest frog, and the smallest of all amphibians, is the Cuban frog, which measures only ⅛ in long. The tiny gold frog, which lives in Brazilian rainforests, is only slightly bigger at about ¾ in (2 cm) long.

Are frogs and toads poisonous?

SOME ARE—THE CANE TOAD CAN SQUIRT POISON AT AN ENEMY FROM GLANDS near its eyes, and the fire-bellied toad has poison in its skin. But most deadly of all are the poison-arrow frogs that live in South American rain forests. Their skin contains one of the most powerful poisons known and a tiny drop can kill a person. Local people tip their hunting arrows with this deadly substance by simply rubbing the arrow over the skin of a frog. Poison-arrow frogs live in trees and are usually very brightly colored. Their bold markings warn predators that they are poisonous and should be left alone. But there is a frog-eating snake in the rain forest that seems to be able to eat the frogs without coming to any harm.

How can treefrogs climb trees?
Treefrogs are excellent climbers. On each of their long toes is a round sticky pad, which allows them to . cling to the undersides of leaves and to run up the smoothest surfaces. Treefrogs spend most of their lives in trees, catching insects to eat, and only come down to the ground to lay their eggs in water.

How did the spadefoot toad get its name?
The spadefoot toad got its name from the hard spadelike projection on each back foot, which it uses for digging its burrow. The toad backs into the ground, pushing soil away with its "spades". It usually spends the day deep in its burrow and comes out at night to find food.

Can the flying frog really fly?

NO, BUT IT CAN GLIDE 40 FT (12 METERS) THROUGH THE AIR BETWEEN TREES.
When the frog jumps into the air it stretches out its legs and toes so that its webbed feet act like little parachutes. Small flaps of skin on the legs also help the frog to glide. The flying frog lives in rain forests in Southeast Asia and spends most of its life in trees. Being able to "fly" in this way means that it does not have to go down to the ground and climb back up again to move from tree to tree.

How many types of frog and toad are there?
There are about 2,500 species of frog and toad. They live on all continents except Antarctica. Most live in areas with plenty of rainfall, but some manage to live in drier lands by sheltering in burrows.

Flaps of skin help the frog glide through the air.

Flying frog

How big is a giant toad?
The giant toad, which lives in parts of the southern United States, is up to 9 ¹/₂ in (24 cm) long. It eats beetles. It has been introduced into many parts of the world by farmers, in an effort to control the beetles that eat crops such as sugarcane.

What is a salamander?
A salamander looks like a lizard with its long body and tail, but it is an amphibian like frogs and toads. There are about 350 different kinds. The biggest is the giant salamander, which can grow to 5 ft (1.5 meters) long.

How can you tell a crocodile from an alligator?

YOU CAN RECOGNIZE A CROCODILE BECAUSE ITS TEETH STICK OUT WHEN ITS MOUTH IS SHUT! In many ways, crocodiles and alligators are very similar. They both have long bodies covered with thick scales. And they both have long jaws with lots of sharp teeth. But when they shut their mouths, there is one difference between them that is easily spotted. In alligators, the fourth pair of teeth on the lower jaw disappears into pits in the upper jaws, but in crocodiles, these teeth slide outside the mouth into notches in the upper jaw, and can be seen when the mouth is closed.

Which is the biggest crocodile?
The Nile crocodile grows up to 19.5 ft (6 meters) long, but the Indopacific crocodile is even larger. This crocodile, which lives in parts of Southeast Asia, grows to 23 ft (7 meters) or more.

Do crocodiles lay eggs?
Crocodiles do lay eggs and they look after them very carefully. The female crocodile digs a pit into which she lays 30 or more eggs. She covers them over with earth or sand. While the eggs incubate for about three months, the female crocodile stays nearby guarding the nest. When the young hatch, the mother hears their cries and lifts them out of the pit with her mouth.

What do crocodiles eat?
Baby crocodiles start by catching insects and spiders to eat. As they grow, fish and birds form a larger part of their diet. Fully grown crocodiles prey on anything that comes their way, even large animals such as giraffes. The crocodile lies in the water near where animals come to drink, then suddenly lurches forward to seize the prey.

How big is a giant tortoise?
Giant tortoises grow up to 4.5 ft (1.4 meters) long and weigh as much as 550 lb (250 kg). They live on the Galapagos Islands in the Pacific and on the island of Aldabra in the Indian Ocean. Seychelles giant tortoises were thought to be extinct in the wild—to have died out completely—but some living animals have recently been discovered. Efforts are being made to breed more tortoises in captivity and release them into the wild.

The green turtle's broad shell is up to 5 ft (1.5 meters) long. Turtles "fly" through the water with the help of their paddle-shaped flippers.

Which is the biggest turtle?
The leatherback is the largest of all the turtles. It grows up to 64 in (1.6 meters) long and weighs up to 794 lb (360 kg). Leatherbacks also dive deeper than other turtles. They plunge down to more than 3,300 ft (1,000 meters).

Green turtle

What do sea turtles eat?
Most sea turtles eat a range of underwater creatures, such as clams, shrimps and snails, but some concentrate on certain foods. The hawksbill is one of the few creatures that feeds mostly on sponges. The leatherback's main food is jellyfish, while the green turtle eats sea grass.

Do turtles ever come to land?

SEA TURTLES SPEND NEARLY ALL THEIR LIVES IN THE WATER, BUT FEMALES do come to land to lay their eggs. The female green turtle drags herself up on to a sandy beach and digs a deep pit. She lays 100 or more eggs and covers them with sand. She then returns to the sea. When the young hatch, they must dig their own way out of the pit and struggle down the beach to the sea. Sadly, many get gobbled up by seabirds and other hunters before they reach the water.

Nile crocodile

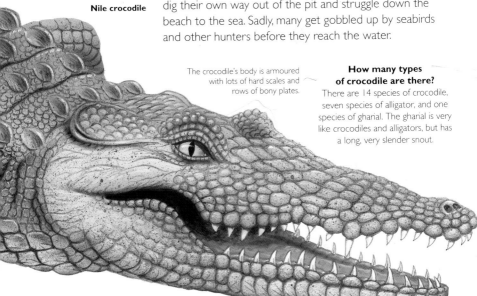

The crocodile's body is armoured with lots of hard scales and rows of bony plates.

How many types of crocodile are there?
There are 14 species of crocodile, seven species of alligator, and one species of gharial. The gharial is very like crocodiles and alligators, but has a long, very slender snout.

25

Which is the most dangerous snake?

The saw-scaled carpet viper is probably the world's most dangerous snake. It is extremely aggressive and its poison can kill humans. Saw-scaled carpet vipers live in Africa and Asia.

How fast do snakes move?

The fastest-moving snake on land is thought to be the black mamba, which lives in Africa. It can wriggle along at up to 12 mph (19 kph).

Which is the largest lizard?

The komodo dragon, which lives on some Southeast Asian islands. It grows up to 10 ft (3 meters) long and hunts animals such as wild pigs and small deer.

Why does a rattlesnake rattle?

Rattlesnakes make their rattling noise to warn their enemies to stay well away. The rattle is made by a number of hard rings of skin at the end of the tail that make a noise when shaken. Each ring was once the tip of the tail. A new one is added every time the snake grows and sheds its skin.

How many kinds of snake are there?

There are about 2,700 species of snake in the world. They live on all continents except Antarctica, but there are no snakes in Ireland, Iceland, or New Zealand. All snakes are carnivorous—that means that they feed on other animals.

Reticulated python

The python can coil its strong body around its prey and crush it to death.

Are there any snakes in the sea?

Yes, there are about 47 different species of snake that spend their whole lives in the sea. Most are completely helpless on land. They eat fish and other sea creatures, such as shrimp, and all are extremely poisonous. One, the beaked sea snake, has the deadliest poison of any snake.

Which is the biggest snake?

THE WORLD'S LONGEST SNAKE IS THE RETICULATED PYTHON, WHICH LIVES IN parts of Southeast Asia. It grows to an amazing 33 ft (10 meters). The anaconda, which lives in South American rain forests, is heavier than the python but not quite as long. Pythons and anacondas are not poisonous snakes. They kill with their teeth or by crushing prey to death. A python lies in wait for its prey, then creeps up and wraps the victim in the powerful coils of its body until it is suffocated.

Are all snakes poisonous?

Only about a third of all snakes are poisonous and fewer still have poison strong enough to harm humans. Nonpoisonous snakes either crush their prey to death or simply swallow it whole.

Why do snakes shed their skin?

Snakes shed their skin, or molt, to allow for growth and because their skin gets worn and damaged. In its first year, when it is growing quickly, a young snake may shed its skin seven times or more. After this, it may only molt once a year or less.

Why does a chameleon change color?

CHANGING COLOR HELPS THE CHAMELEON GET NEAR ITS PREY without being seen and allows it to hide from its own enemies. The color change is controlled by the chameleon's nervous system. Nerves cause areas of color in the skin to be spread out or to become concentrated in tiny dots. Chameleons are also said to go darker in color when angry and lighter when afraid.

Chameleon

Are there any poisonous lizards?
There are only two poisonous lizards in the world—the gila monster and the Mexican beaded lizard, both of which live in western North America. The poison is made in glands in the lower jaw. When the lizard seizes a prey and starts to chew, poison flows into the wound. Overpowered by the poison, the victim soon stops struggling.

Where do chameleons live?
There are about 85 different sorts of chameleon and most of these live in Africa and Madagascar. There are a few Asian species and one kind of chameleon lives in parts of southern Europe.

How many kinds of lizard are there?
There are about 3,000 different species of lizard. These belong to different groups, or families, such as the geckos, iguanas, skinks, and chameleons. There are lizards on all continents, except Antarctica, but most live in warm parts of the world.

The python's jaws open extremely wide so it can swallow prey larger than itself.

Do all penguins live in Antarctica?

Most of the 18 species of penguin live in or near Antarctica, but some are found in warmer areas. There are several species around New Zealand, one in the tropical Galapagos Islands and one on South African coasts. There are no penguins in the northern hemisphere.

Which is the smallest penguin?

The little, or fairy, penguin is the smallest penguin – it is only about 16 in (40 cm) long. It lives in waters off the coasts of New Zealand and Tasmania.

Emperor penguins

Which is the biggest penguin?

THE EMPEROR LIVES IN ANTARCTICA, AND IS THE BIGGEST PENGUIN THE WORLD.

It stands about 37 in (95 cm) tall. Like all penguins, the emperor cannot fly, but it is an expert swimmer and diver, using its wings as paddles. It spends most of its life in the water, where it catches fish and squid to eat. Emperor penguins do come to land to breed. The female lays one egg, which the male bird then keeps warm on his feet. The female goes back to the sea, but the male stays and incubates the egg for about 60 days. He cannot leave it, even to feed. The female returns when the egg hatches and cares for the chick while the starving male goes to find food.

What is a tropicbird?

A tropicbird is a seabird with two very long central tail feathers. There are three species, all of which fly over tropical oceans.

The emperor penguin has waterproof feathers and a thick layer of fat to keep out the cold of Antarctica.

28

Which bird makes the longest migration?

The Arctic tern makes the longest migration journey of any bird. Each year it makes a round trip of more than 25,000 miles (40,000 km). The birds nest in the Arctic in the northern summer and then travel south to spend the southern summer near Antarctica, where food is plentiful.

Why does a pelican have a pouch?

The pelican has a pouch to help it catch fish to eat. When the bird plunges its open beak into the water the pouch fills up with water and fish. As it brings its head up again, the water drains from the pouch, leaving any fish behind to be swallowed.

How many kinds of gull are there?

There are about 45 species of gull. They live in all parts of the world, but there are more species north of the equator. Gulls range in size from the little gull, which is only 11 (28 cm) long, to the great black-backed gull, a huge 26 in (65 cm) long. Many gulls find food inland as well as at sea and some even scavenge in towns and cities.

How does a gannet catch its food?

The gannet catches fish and squid in spectacular dives into the sea. This graceful seabird flies over the water looking for prey. When it sees something, it plunges from as high as 100 ft (30 meters) above the ocean, dives into the water with its wings swept back and seizes the catch in its daggerlike beak.

Is a puffin a kind of penguin?

No, puffins belong to a different family of birds, called auks. They live in the northern hemisphere, particularly around the Arctic. Auks are good swimmers and divers, like penguins, but they can also fly.

Wandering albatross

The wandering albatross has a strong hooked beak that helps it catch its slippery prey.

Can all seabirds swim?

Not all seabirds can swim. Frigatebirds cannot swim and avoid going into the water. They seize food from the surface or rob other birds of their catches. Storm petrels, too, rarely land on the water, preferring to swoop close to the surface.

Which bird has the longest wings?

THE WANDERING ALBATROSS HAS THE LONGEST WINGS OF ANY LIVING BIRD. When fully spread they measure up to 11 ft (3.3 meters) from tip to tip. This majestic seabird spends much of its life soaring over the ocean far from land and it may travel several hundred miles a day. It lays its eggs and cares for its young on islands near Antarctica.

Can all cormorants fly?

There are about 30 different kinds of cormorant and all but one can fly. The flightless cormorant lives in the Galapagos Islands off the coast of South America. It has tiny wings and cannot fly, but it is an expert swimmer. It catches all of its food in the water.

How fast do penguins swim?

Penguins have been timed swimming at speeds of 6 mph (10 kph), but may move even faster for short periods. They can dive under water for two minutes or more. Emperors are believed to be able to stay under water for more than 18 minutes.

Harpy eagle

The harpy eagle has shorter wings than other eagles so that it can fly among the branches of rain forest trees.

Which is the fastest flying bird?

As it dives to catch other birds in the air, the peregrine falcon may move at more than 100 mph (160 kph), faster than any other bird. The falcon circles above its victim before making its fast dive and killing the prey with a blow from its powerful talons.

Do eagles build nests?

Yes, and the nest made by the bald eagle is the biggest made by any bird. Some bald eagle nests are up to 18 ft (5.5 meters) deep. They are used again and again and the eagles add more nest material each year.

What does an osprey eat?

The osprey feeds mostly on fish. When it sees something near the surface, it dives down towards the water and seizes the fish in its feet. The soles of its feet are covered with small spines to help it hold on to the slippery fish.

Which is the biggest eagle?

THE BIGGEST EAGLE IN THE WORLD IS THE HARPY EAGLE, WHICH LIVES IN RAIN FORESTS in South America. It is up to 43 in (110 cm) long and has huge feet and sharp talons, which it uses to kill its prey. Unlike other eagles, the harpy does not soar high in the air looking for food. It hunts creatures such as monkeys and sloths in the trees, chasing its victims from branch to branch at high speed. Almost as big is the rare Philippine monkey-eating eagle, which lives in rain forests in the Philippines.

Bearded vultures gathering at a carcass

The bearded vulture gets its name from the clump of black bristles that hangs under its beak.

Which is the biggest bird of prey?

The Andean condor is the the biggest bird of prey in the world. It measures up to 43 in (110 cm) long and weighs up to 25 lb (12 kg). Its wingspan is over 10 ft (3 meters).

How do eagles kill their prey?

An eagle kills with the four long curved claws on each of its feet. It drops down on to the victim, seizes it in its long talons and crushes it to death. The eagle then tears the flesh apart with its strong hooked beak. The hook of a golden eagle's beak is as much as 4 in (10 cm) long.

Do eagles really catch snakes?

Yes, serpent eagles feed mostly on snakes and lizards. The rough surface of the serpent eagle's toes helps it hold on to slippery snakes.

How many kinds of owl are there?

There are about 142 different species of owl in two different families. The barn owl family contains about 12 species and the true owl family about 130 species. Owls live in most parts of the world, except a few islands. They usually hunt at night, catching small mammals, birds, frogs, lizards, insects, and even fish.

How can owls hunt at night?

Owls have excellent sight, even in low light, and extremely sharp hearing. Even in complete darkness they can pinpoint where a sound is coming from and swoop. Owls also have special soft-edged wing feathers which make very little noise as they beat their wings. This allows them to approach prey with scarcely a sound.

Do vultures hunt and kill prey?

VULTURES DO NOT USUALLY KILL THEIR PREY. THEY ARE SCAVENGERS, FEEDING on animals that are already dead or have been killed by hunters such as lions. They have strong claws and beaks and the bald head allows them to plunge into carcasses without dirtying their feathers. The bearded vulture, or lammergeier, often picks up bones, which it drops on to rocks to smash them open. It can then feed on the marrow inside.

The bearded vulture soars on its long narrow wings high over remote mountains in parts of southern Europe, Asia, and Africa

Index